# MY PERSPECTIVE

For permission requests, write to the publisher, addressed "Attention: Permissions Coordinator," 205 N. Michigan Avenue, Suite #810, Chicago, IL 60601. 13th & Joan books may be purchased for educational, business or sales promotional use. For information, please email the Sales Department at sales@13thandjoan.com.

Printed in the U. S. A.

First Printing, September 2023.

Library of Congress Cataloging-in-Publication Data has been applied for.

ISBN: 978-1-953156-94-5

# MY PERSPECTIVE

AUTHORED BY ZADA N. LUBY

# ENDORSEMENTS

Powerful. Poignant. Purpose-filled. Zada Luby's *My Perspective* carries the reader on a literary journey through her stream of consciousness from her earliest childhood memories to her current life as a teenager and budding young adult. While reading her book, I was drawn into her detailed ability to chronicle her life experiences and simultaneously blown away by the impactful manner in which she dissects and processes her emotions, feelings and reactions during each stage of her development. With the natural nuances of an African Griot, she takes the reader with her through some of her most painful moments and glorious accomplishments in her 18 years of life. Yet, the silver lining of her story is the understated hero she found in her father, Zeus. Their relationship becomes the cornerstone of her resiliency and the key to unlocking the powerful potential he always knew was inside of her. This book will change the lives not only of young adults, but it will transform the way parents and caretakers view their responsibilities to their children. *My Perspective* is a remarkable and beautiful story for all audiences and ages, but especially for those who are needing a tale of inspiration fueled by the perseverance of one young woman, combined with the unwavering love of a father, who together, despite all odds, refused to succumb to the pressures of self-doubt and external sabotage; and instead rose to the pinnacles of self-realization, self-worth and self-love.

– Respectfully, Dr. Lattisha Bilbrew

From the first word you read until the book's closing, the honesty in which Zada Luby shares her life story pulls you in and captivates you. As a fellow writer, I was in awe of her ability to reach into such a vulnerable and intimate space and compose a book so eloquently written at such a young age. In a society that seems to have lost its sense of community, *My Perspective* is a relatable body of work that will inspire young women who may have otherwise felt isolated. I enjoyed every minute of reading *My Perspective* and will be recommending it to all the young women I know.

– Stephanie Ogbogu – Writer, Journalist

This book is a preview into the masterful unfolding of a young lady who will take her humble beginnings and create purpose and offer promise to all of those who watch her blossom. I was blown away by Zada's high-level of communication at age 15-18 to write such a book. To be this honest and aware at such a young age is a gift to those of all ages who will read it. The most beautiful part of the story is a rough start can still lead to a beautiful ending. If you've felt like an underdog or been bullied, this story will encourage you to keep living; it will all get better at the end. However, this is far from the ending of Zada's story. I'm excited for her next book already!

— Brely Evans, Actress

# DEDICATION

This book is dedicated to my family and my extended village, Trelita Goins, Jael Roberson, Che Bledsoe, Jennifer Young, Donald & Janice Murphy, Hosea Chanchez, Karen Blackwell, Tamisha Woods, Tenesha Sellers, Stephanie Ogbogu, Treya Tolbert, Kayla Shelton, Naturi Noughton, Angela Bassett, Anthony Hemingway, Dexter Davis, Kendria Johnson, Brandon Thaxton, Octavius Terry, and Andre Hilton. Everyone above has aided in my journey, and I appreciate all of you so much. All of you mean more to me than I can put into words! Last, but definitely not least, thank you to my father, Zeus Luby. You are my hero, big brother, and my best friend. Thank you for always being there for me and staying strong and patient despite the hardships and woeful times. Not only could I have not accomplished any of my aspirations without you, but I also wouldn't be here without you. For that, not only do I dedicate this book to you, but also my entire life.

# EPIGRAPH

" Turn your wounds
into wisdom

— OPRAH WINFREY

# FOREWORD

Meet Zada Luby, a robust, vastly consummate, altruistic young lady who overcame her past experiences and used them as the building blocks for a better future. Her goal in life is to use her story to help others conquer their own hardships. Beyond that, whilst working to quell the adverse effects of her quondam situation, she's embarked on a slue of endeavors to change her life and make a name for herself. From a young age, Ms. Luby was interested in the arts. She always found herself drawing, singing, or trying to imitate her favorite television characters. Once presented, at the age of eleven, with the unique opportunity of attending Brandon Thaxton's acting classes, Acting Up Atlanta, she gleefully jumped at the idea. Unbeknownst to her, this opportunity would get her picked up by an agency and completely change her life.

A year later Ms. Luby would book her first role as the lead in the independent film, *Ruth*, starring alongside the incredibly gifted Hosea Chanchez and Naturi Naughton. Later that year, using her demo reel from her previous work she'd be featured on NewsNation's *The Underground*, acting opposite the prodigious Angela Bassett. It was a riveting event in her life that helped fuel the fervor she had for acting even more. Concomitantly, she pursued another passion of hers. A perfervid fashionmonger, she expressed an exceptional interest in clothing design. She started attending weekly lessons to develop and hone her sewing skill. With the help of her teacher, Karen Kice, remarkably adroit in her craft and founder of Karen Kice Collections, she was able to design pieces she'll not only keep forever, but some of which she still wears to this day.

Ms. Luby is also a sketch artist. She's been illustrating since she was four. Her love of art stems from a common dexterity of creative physical expression threaded throughout her lineage. From pictures of people to pictures of crashed spaceships, what she drew was not confined to any set parameters. As she continued to practice, as if she had planted a seed, her gift soon blossomed to the point of which, by the time she was fifteen, she had been commissioned to illustrate a specifc piece for a client. Now, Ms. Luby continues to do sketch art to perfect her gift.

Above all else, Ms. Luby is a proud and doting daughter of her father, Zeus Luby. He is her biggest inspiration and role model. Ms. Luby strives to emulate her father's tenacity, benevolence, magnanimity, and buoyancy. Her father is her world and she attributes much of her triumph to her father being by her side every step of the way. This book tells the story about Ms. Luby leading up to the life she currently lives and dives deeper into her inner thoughts throughout the journey she took to get here. This book gives insight into how she's overcome her past obstacles and repurposed them for fuel towards her current reality. Her story could help those who have gone through similar experiences by showing them that they're not alone in what they've had to endure and that there are others who have not only shared the same thoughts during such situations, but have also made the same mistakes as a result. This will help others understand that healing is possible and just within everyone's reach. Her story serves as a valuable read to anyone who has fallen victim to a similar state of affairs.

# CONTENTS

# PREFACE

The intentions behind the contents of this book are rooted in my own desire to have a story to relate to. The following details my own true thoughts and experiences as an innocent child subjected to witnessing the unfortunate separation of my parents and having to bear the brunt of my mother's carelessness, emotional and mental manipulation, and neglect. The ultimate goal is to provide a piece of relatable media to those who've fallen victim to similar circumstances. I vividly remember being so bewildered; suddenly the foundation of everything I'd come to know shifted, as if I'd been standing on an active fault line the entire time. I'd like others to find refuge and comfort in the varying aspects of my story that resonate with them.

# INTRODUCTION

This book invites you to peer into a harrowing journey of the past. Whilst her father fights tooth and nail for the sake of his daughter's wellbeing, the little girl finds herself fighting her own internal battle. Armed with nothing but hope, she finds herself navigating the duplicitous treachery of her mother. In the end, though distressing, she sees the light at the end of the tunnel and runs into the arms of her hero, the man who saved her from the rubble after her entire world came tumbling down.

**P**EOPLE SAY I SWIM LIKE A FISH, and yet, a part of me has been drowning for fifteen years. At times, I feel like I'm about to break through the water and finally be welcomed by the fresh air I've been missing out on. However, when I look in the mirror, I'm reminded that I'm drowning and I'm back where I started. I tear up as I think about how I look just like her, and how I act like her. On October 27, 2003, I was welcomed into the world. In 2005, my mother kicked me and my dad out to make room for her new life. Though she immediately realized she had exchanged a huge loss for a small gain, she was unable to redeem herself. My dad was done with her and her games.

Now ineligible to be a picture-perfect family, we were added to the thousands of broken ones, and I was subjected to being tossed back and forth between two homes. It was almost like a job, putting on a smile to keep both of my parents happy; only my briefcase and documents were replaced by my travel bag filled with clothes and toiletries.

My young age blinded everyone to the possibility that I understood the abnormality of my situation. My surroundings and experiences were very different from the ones I saw on television. My favorite shows were filled with happy families, eating and laughing together, while my reality was the complete opposite. I was hit with a whirlwind of evidence that my life was nothing short of atypical. All five of my senses became unusually familiar with public transportation: the musty metallic smell, the flickering lights, and the ripped seams on the bus seats. The uncomfortable absence of both my parents at the pick-up desk, compared to my pre-k classmates whose moms and dads would always be there to greet them with two sets of reassuring arms, also became all too familiar. Whenever I was out and about, everywhere I looked, whether the child was an infant or a high schooler, it just seemed like they always had both parents with them. The loneliness I felt was so strong, I could smell it. I always had an affinity for soft, flowery smells, but this smell was pungent and overbearing. It lingered in the air around me, but only when I thought about how my parents weren't together. I started dismissing my thoughts, and as those thoughts faded so, too, did the smell. For a while, I felt calm and light, like weights were lifted off my shoulders. No longer did my throat feel sore from holding back my tears. I finally attained a peaceful state of mind.

This feeling faded quickly. Soon, things went back to the way they were. My body got heavier, my throat once again became sore, and my life became dark. While I thought I was doing myself a favor by pushing my feelings down, I was just hurting myself even more. I didn't realize my feelings would take me down with them. At this time, I felt like I was imprisoned by my own thoughts. Every ounce of hope I had drained from my body.

To top it all off, my mother did nothing to help my clearly detrimental situation. She would torment me with her fake tears; an attempt to get me to feel guilty for leaving her to visit my dad. As if I had a choice in who I was with at what time. She'd con me every seven days into believing that my dad was trying to keep me from seeing her and into feeling sorry for her.

Blind to my pain, she was partially to blame for the downward spiral my mind went through. A plethora of emotions ran rampant through my thoughts as she sat back and watched my mental state deteriorate.

My inability to understand my own emotions caused them to overpower and consume me completely, until I was no longer myself. The way I felt manifested into my behavior and turned me into a troubled child that no one felt like dealing with. My patience became very short and my temper became more problematic. Instead of using words, I resolved my issues with physical tactics that warded off not just foe, but friends just as well.

After I established a reputation of violence, my friends started to steer clear of me. I'd wonder, what's wrong with me? Why don't they want to play with me? Questions such as these fogged my brain almost every day. Everything got even worse. I felt like an outcast. With this, my temper worsened, and pre-school became a living hell. The caretakers of my pre-school dealt with my behavior poorly, having little to no interest in hearing my side. Little did I know, my situation was about to escalate even more. My mother was determined to have me all to herself, and she had her mind set on trying every legal method possible to achieve this goal—a decision that pushed my dad to near insanity and caused other family members to drop to their knees praying for my protection and care. She kept me from my dad and his side of my family for two months without any valid explanation. The start of those two months was one of the worst periods of my life, as my dad had the only key to my happiness.

By this time, my mother had already bounced around to four different houses since my dad moved out. The fourth home was where I spent that torturous two months away from my dad, and it would be the last home I'd ever live in with my mother. Given how frequently she relocated, there was never an opportunity to plant roots, leaving no history or memories there to comfort me. The house wasn't homey, bright, or inviting, and where I lived, children were scarce. There was hardly anything to disturb the melancholy feeling that overwhelmed me. Until the house from across the street was revealed to be inhabited by a friendly family of one mom and four boys. Three out of those four boys, though all fond of me, were too old for me to really play with. The youngest of them was six and I was five. We clicked instantly and our relationship blossomed into a close friendship.

Once again, I was greeted with peace during a desolate time in my life, but, unlike before, my happiness stretched beyond what I imagined it would.

My longing for my dad never subsided, the excitement of a new friend crowded my mind, making it very hard for anything else to grab my attention. All aspects of my life got better. Since my mood shifted, my friends gravitated to me once again, and my mental health seemed that of a normal child with a bright future.

Everything was going great, except for my physical health. In the past, while my mother got a chance to do whatever she wanted with me within her seven-day time slot, my dad had to play doctor. My mother lacked basic culinary skills and seemed to be aware that even in comparison to cheap, fast food, hers wasn't ideal. So, due to her ignorance of how to feed a fragile, five-year-old body; every day for breakfast, lunch, and dinner, she fed me loads of fat and empty calories.

My body would grow weak, and whenever I was sent to my dad's house, I was unable to use the bathroom and my weight was below the average for my age. She would also send me back to my dad with a knotty and dirty head of hair. When I was younger, my hair was short and hard to manage. Even so, my dad was able to style it fairly well, while my mother, on the other hand, had no idea what to do when it came to my hair. She'd put it up in these painfully tight knots that started to pull out my baby hairs, and at times, pulled out even more than that.

Even though I was too distracted to notice, things clearly still weren't working out in my favor, but they were working out in my mother's. During this two-month period, the only time my mother reached out to my dad was to tell him that he wouldn't see me again, then a custody battle ensued. Thus, the gates of hell were opened. Of course, during the battle, more stress would be accumulated, which would only add to my dad's already crippling load. In addition to the obvious issue of legal expenses, the greater dilemma was knowing that during such a battle, women usually have the upper hand. So, even though my mother shouldn't win, from the beginning, she had a much greater chance at victory. That alone almost ensured that I was destined to have an atrocious fate.

While my parents fought to change my living situation, I enjoyed my friend. Over time I became part of his family—to his older brothers, I was a little sister, and to his mom, a daughter. I'd frequently go over to his house and sometimes I even spent the night. As the days went by, we grew closer and closer, but we seemed to be getting a little too close.

At times, when I'd be lying down on my couch, he'd get next to me and lay with me, and sometimes when I'd spend the night we'd sleep in the same bed. Though kids that aren't related sleep in the same bed all the time, one thing in particular happened that made it apparent that certain lines were being crossed. One day, he came over to my house to play. We went into my room and closed the door. My mother opened it so she could see what we were doing. She stayed in a different room, which was at a reasonable distance to keep us in sight. After a back and forth debate we decided on playing dress up, since that was my favorite thing to play. As I got dressed into my princess outfit, he tried to peek, but my mother told him to go on the other side of my bed and crouch down so he wouldn't be able to see me. Once I was dressed, we played and played for hours. When we were done, he made a request that I didn't quite understand at the time. He calmly asked if I would pull down my pants. I stared at him for a second in confusion. After checking for my mother, only to find that we were unattended, and closing the door, I proceeded to do as he asked. He then asked me to pull down my underwear. Not at all appalled at this request, I once again stared at him and then proceeded to do as he asked. Then he followed suit. Not comprehending what he was doing, or how it was to be properly done, what happened after, didn't leave me without my virginity. But his requests didn't end there. After we were both fully clothed again, he asked if he could kiss me, specifically on the most intimate area of my face. Though I was hesitant, I agreed to do it anyway. And after the first kiss, many more followed.

After our experience we walked out of my room like nothing happened, and for the rest of the day, though we felt awkward, no one outside of the two of us seemed to know. The next day, already feeling nervous, I dreaded the fact that I was going over to his house. I was greeted by a question that sent my heart into a tailspin. While I was outside playing with him, his oldest brother asked us if we had kissed. I stood frozen with fear as he stared at us with an expression that demanded an answer. Then his younger brother revealed our secret with no hesitation.

The news quickly traveled from his lips, to his older brother, to his entire family, and my mother. I didn't get in trouble, but our time together definitely decreased moving forward. By this time, I had already gotten back to my normal routine and I was able to see my dad and the rest of my family. Of course, with the tension instilled by my mother between the two sides of my family, the news never got to them. With them being left in the dark and no one taking any action, I was left by my lonesome to deal with the embarrassment and discomfort. I'd replay that incident over and over in my mind, rewinding and stopping it at different parts, dissecting it to get a better understanding. After a while, it didn't matter as much.

In time, my friend and I were able to see one another more, and no one ever bought up the incident. Even as tense as I was, eventually I managed to calm down and ease my mind. Things finally seemed to be moving at a steady pace. I hoped it would continue that way. Like it was mentioned earlier, my mother kicked me and my dad out a year after I was born. Her reason for doing so was to be with the man she had been cheating on my dad with previously. While the custody battle was going on, he was living there. When I was younger, he seemed just as nice as any other adult. He didn't shout at me and I don't recall any time he hit me. Apparently, he was capable of such things and more. Sadly, I found this out the hard way. Not too long after the incident I had with my friend, I found myself involved in something even more serious. I'm unable to remember what her boyfriend did to me, but I do vividly remember my mother threatening to hurt me if I were to say anything about it. Because of my age, I didn't understand his actions. So of course, my first thought wasn't to dial 911 or to call anyone else that had a significant authority over him. Though something should've been done right then, nothing happened immediately. Nothing he could've done frightened me the same way my mother's threat did.

This is probably the only time I can think of where I was truly scared for my life, and as I thought about it more, I became overwhelmed with sadness. I couldn't fathom the thought of my mother actually having the desire to inflict pain on me. During this time, fear was the most prominent feeling I had. I was so worried that I might accidentally tell someone what happened. I felt if that were to ever happen, my mother would just come out of nowhere and start doing as she said. Her words terrorized me every day. No matter where I was, I started applying what she said to the way I handled people. I started to get short with my responses when talking to friends and I started to distance myself from family members. For a while at least, my mind was at ease while I was asleep. After a while, even my dreams were heavily affected. Every night, almost instantly after my head would hit the pillow, I was engulfed into a world where every encounter with my mother consisted of her causing me some form of pain. However, my pain would soon be over.

As my mother caused drama at home, she also managed to do the same in the courtroom. On top of the fact that she got more support during the case just for being my mother, she also sold lie after lie to the judge, which paved an easy way to her victory. Luckily, I had two secrets that could make this case take a sharp turn. One day, while I was with my dad, I asked him if it was bad to kiss boys. As that conversation progressed, I confessed what took place between me and my friend. To get all the details of that situation, I was required, by the court, to go to counseling. In counseling, not only did I give further detail about that situation, but I also explained what my mother's boyfriend did to me and how my mother threatened to hurt me if I told anyone about it.

With that information, and a lawyer that continued to fight despite my dad's shortage of money, my dad ultimately won the case and my mother's boyfriend was thrown in jail. Even though justice was served, and I was being saved from the hell my mother had been putting me through, I was absolutely devastated. Once my dad won the case, my grandmother came to get me, but it was my last time anyone would be picking me up from my mother's house and I was aware of that. All I can remember is my grandmother having to pry me away from my mother's arms and just about force me into the car. Even though I had officially started life without my mother, I still had an array of issues that followed me years down the line.

Leaving my mother's house felt like my life was completely starting over. I left behind my preschool, my best friend, and my mother. Due to the severity of the situations that took place while I was in her care, I was unable to have any form of contact with her. For a long time after I left, when memories of her resurfaced, they'd linger in my mind for hours and hours. As a child, I didn't know of any proper way to deal with my emotions, so a lot of my frustrations came out through my behavior.

When I would get upset about something I couldn't fix, I would throw and hit things until I was either stopped or it broke. Sometimes when something wasn't doing what I wanted it to do I would aggressively talk to it and threaten to break it unless it did as I asked. In school I would handle people the same way. When someone would do things that provoked me, I would retaliate with violence. Due to the emotional trauma, I also made things really hard for my dad. I was convinced that he was the reason my mother was no longer around, so for a while I resented him. I would lie to him and I didn't communicate with him like a father and daughter should. It also took him a long time to gain my trust. Regardless, he continued to work with me.

He took me to countless counselors. He also took the time to explain to me why something I did was wrong. He approached the situation diligently. Within a year, I had transformed into a sweet, pure little girl. Even though it might not have seemed that way, I still had plenty of problems. My agony followed me like a shadow. Over time, having to bear such heavy emotions crippled me. I became very reclusive and shy. I also had severe confidence issues that impaired my ability to make friends. Walking through the door of my first kindergarten classroom, the first thing I did was look around and compare myself to every single one of my classmates. I would look to find those who were prettier than me and those who might've been smarter than me. From then on, wherever I went, I'd compare myself. Because I was afraid of my "competition" I tried to keep as much distance as I possibly could, and due to how selective and reclusive I was, I didn't have a slew of friends like most kids do at that age.

When I started comparing the amount of friends I had to the amount others would have,

I started feeling like something was wrong with me. I would immediately blame it on my looks and my intelligence. Through my eyes, the most popular kids were also the most attractive and got the best grades on everything. At some point, my doubt made me feel almost unworthy. Most of my friends were comrades of friends I already had. I wouldn't have ever ventured out on my own looking for friends. I felt most people wouldn't enjoy my company, so I just let them come as they did.

My lack of popularity made me feel inferior and unimportant. Though I didn't hate myself, I did dislike a lot of things about myself. I also found myself trying to change a lot of those things and imitate those I envied, and the things I did like about myself, I tried to highlight more. As time went by, my confidence plummeted even more.

Though I had academic trouble in kindergarten, I understood enough to achieve my 'Principal's List' goal, but first grade had a little less leeway when it came to the grading system. Math and language arts were my mortal enemies, which were the two most important of the four main subjects. While my classmates would raise their hands high in excitement, I stayed quiet and buried my head in my arms as an attempt to hide. Due to the lackluster pre-school my mother had me in when I was younger, I was behind, and I had no confidence in my academic ability. First grade was already a challenge because of my low confidence, but then on top of that, school got increasingly harder throughout the year. As my classes became more challenging, my grades started to go down. I found myself freezing up on math tests and still reading at a kindergarten level. I started to think of myself as unintelligent and I often compared myself to mentally disabled children. After a few months I became immensely frustrated with myself and my poor performance.

It became clear to me that even though my dad never showed his feelings directly, he wasn't too proud of my grades. I felt like a burden. I always needed help with my homework and sometimes he had to completely reteach things to me. Whenever I attempted to try my hand at the work myself, I'd always get frustrated and give up. If I got too flustered, sometimes, I would break down into tears and throw tantrums. Already at the tender age of seven, I reached a level of stress beyond my years. In addition to the trouble I had with school, I had even more to endure at home.

Not only did I have episodic and uncontrolled bursts of bottled up emotions, but the dreams that harassed me before crept their way back into my mind. No matter how my day panned out, it always ended the same. Throughout the nights, I would sweat and cry uncontrollably, while in my dreams I'd be running from my mother as she chased me with an axe. Some nights were so bad I'd wake up screaming and throwing up. Though the dreams were terrifying on their own, one of the worst parts about them were the memories that accompanied them. Horrifically graphic and realistic nightmares poisoned my sleep and my life by reminding me of distasteful memories of my solemn past. Memories that I purposely discarded resurfaced as my nightmares recurred. Even as terrible as my dreams already were, there was still room for them to get much worse. Because my mother was no longer around, what I feared the most, and still fear to this day, is my dad being taken out of my life. My already traumatizing dreams got even darker once images of my dad getting brutally murdered were added. Due to how young I was and how realistic they were, every time I had a night terror such as that, I thought it was real. For a while my dad had a night job where he was working as a security guard. Once he told me what his job meant, that only fueled my fear. I was now afraid for him when I was conscious and while I was asleep. When he'd come home later than usual, my paranoia would drive me mad. Making me consider all the things that could've happened to him, and a life without him. These were the thoughts that controlled my emotions until he walked through the front door. While I was revisited by these memories, health issues from my past also resurfaced.

Most might agree that I was born into a pretty unfortunate situation, but more than just my parents separating characterized it as such. Before I got to see my first birthday, I almost took my last breath due to asthma. As most are aware, there are a multitude of things that can cause an attack. A few months after I was born, I started having significant problems with my breathing. Due to the severity of my asthma, I had to take regular medicated breathing treatments to regulate my flare ups. But despite the medication, the complications persisted. After countless doctors failed to pinpoint the root of the problem, my dad did extensive research of his own, but even then, the source of the issue remained anonymous. This led to regular trips to the emergency room, making it more and more difficult for doctors to bring stability to my respiratory patterns. This mounting chaos culminated in one fateful ER visit, where the normally lung-soothing medication failed to take effect. After multiple rounds of meds, and hours of me struggling to breathe, it seemed I was running out of time. I lay gasping miserably for air in my mother's arms, as the doctor broke the heart-wrenching news that my chances of survival were slim. From my mother on down to the doctor, a domino effect of tears followed the crushing revelation. In an attempt to save me, they admitted me and placed me on a respirator.

The hospital staff didn't think I would pull through. And even if I did, if the cause of my attacks wasn't pinpointed, I'd eventually relapse after being released and subsequently die. My dad was determined to find the culprit of my health woes. He rushed out of the hospital in a rage and headed back home in feverish pursuit of the cause for my asthmatic episodes. After racking his brain for hours, he finally discovered it. What appeared to be small cracks in the paint near the baseboards of our house turned out to be mold. Upon realizing this, my dad tore through the apartment and found mold covering the shoes and clothes in our closets and blanketing the underside of his and my mother's bed. That deadly mold is what I was unwittingly breathing in day in and day out as I crawled across those poisonous carpets, setting off my dreadful flare-ups. After this revelation and threats of lawsuits against the complex, we moved, and I reverted back to my healthy, bubbly, infant self. Even though that specific issue with my asthma was extinguished, this became just another complication that would follow me down the line.

Like most kids, I enjoyed typical outdoor activities, most of which required the cardiovascular endurance of the average child, but because of my asthma, I had limits that when reached, caused me great discomfort, frustration, and fear. Due to my trouble breathing, my chest often felt like it was collapsing, which caused me to feel like I was dying. With my asthmatic complications and ignorance to how common my condition was, I started revisiting the same problem of feeling abnormal and out of place. I was well aware of my innumerable visits to the hospital and felt that couldn't be normal. And yes, going to the hospital relieved me of my pain and discomfort, but I was tired of being a child of high maintenance and always feeling like the sick little girl. I just wanted a sense of normalcy that I felt I never had. On my search for an average life, I felt lost and alone. Alone, because it seemed like no one else I knew had to go on this same journey, and lost, because I didn't know where to look. I felt like a sickly child who's second home was the doctor's office, and I felt like it would stay that way for the rest of my life. Thankfully, I had a gift that could take my mind off of all my stress.

Before I was unable to see my mother, my dad exposed me to the beautiful world of art. Being the origin of my talent, my dad equipped me with all the tools every artist on the rise needs. I started off with a drawing pad. My imagination ran away with the idea of being able to bring my thoughts to life. The unlimited possibilities of what I could create mesmerized me, and I developed a deep love for art. In school, I used drawing when I was bored and when there were assignments that required artistic ability, but at home, when I wasn't working on perfecting my skill, I often made drawing an outlet for my bottled-up pain. While normally it took a while for me to decide what I wanted to draw, when I took my emotions into account, ideas would flow out of me like water. When coming home from school—like my thoughts—my drawings went from light to dark. I started off drawing pictures of my mother and I holding hands and just being happy together. Throughout different stages of my life, different memories regarding my past situation clouded my thoughts. This was contingent upon how far along I was with my recovery process. At this point in my life, I was in a stage of denial, I refused to believe that my right to see my mother was revoked. So, being in such a mindset, my thoughts often wandered off and took me back to happier times. Back to times I wanted to relive but couldn't. The times when I wasn't drawing me and my mother, I was off drawing dismal comics in dark solitude.

While I would be drawing pictures of blithe times from my past, other memories would invade my peaceful thoughts, taunting them with fleeting glee, stricken down by unfortunate incidents. I started developing ideas for comics, and consistently placed myself as the main character. I would always start off really happy in the beginning, but as the story progressed the plot got darker and darker. Usually resulting in the death of my dad. Looking back, I never understood why I got such pleasure out of creating such sadistic stories. I'd like to think it was due to my deep fear of his demise, but I often killed him myself in my comics as well. In fact, he often played the antagonist, where his character would keep me from my mother, and I would fight back. I revisited this topic a number of times, with the plot always consisting of my dad being killed. This recurring theme of comics was short lived. Like most kids, my amusement moved toward lighthearted children's shows, and I became infatuated with lovable characters like SpongeBob. Though, eventually I'd stop using my art as a coping mechanism, I continued drawing at school.

It became something I did less for myself and more for teachers and friends. My peers fell in love with my art style and my teachers were impressed with my ability. Drawing became somewhat of a party trick. Due to my talent, I was accepted into the realm of true popularity. My artwork gave me a sense of purpose and importance. Not only was I popular, but my ability was always in high demand, and I was often sought after by those who wished to learn to draw. Though I still continued to have problems at home, because of school, I felt I had it made. I had infinite friends, my teachers liked me, there were no serious problems. Nothing else mattered, at least that's what I assumed. But my dad made sure to remind me that even at eight years old, I had responsibilities.

Science and social studies took little effort to pass with an eighty or above, but I still had complications with math and language arts. No matter how hard I tried, I couldn't seem to grasp any of the concepts that we learned. So, I figured it wouldn't do me any good to keep trying for something that was never going to happen. I stopped paying attention and I started cheating on work and tests in class, thinking that was the only way I would pass. But my method of passing was flawed. I never got caught cheating, but while my classwork grades flourished, my test grades suffered even more severely than before. Given that test results were more than half of my overall grade, I started falling just below a B. I went on to the next grade with the same problems as before. I felt like I failed myself and my dad. Since I was older, he started expressing his feelings about my grades and handling me with a heavy hand. My desire to make him proud fueled my drive in class. Despite my motivation, by the end of fourth grade, my average in math still fell a few points short of my goal. The tantrums I threw due to my poor grades got more dramatic and became more frequent. My envy toward those with a better GPA grew as well. My hope for doing better started dissipating, until every ounce was completely gone. My doubt regarding my intellect spilled over into every other aspect of my daily life. Stupid, ignorant, and foolish were words that pounded in my head with every error or mistake I made. These words rang even louder once my peers started basing the level of respect I deserved on my performance in class.

The other students treated me like an airhead and excluded me from doing work during group assignments. They also felt the topics I enjoyed talking about were unworthy of discussion and would possibly infect their intellectual conversations. So, even if they didn't mean to, they ultimately belittled me and made me feel unfit to be friends with anyone I considered to be intelligent. As days, weeks, and months went by, I dug myself deeper and deeper into a hole of endless sorrow and shame. Fifth grade didn't seem like it would have much more to offer. My grades were still low, and I was still being treated like I was less than. Finally, I did meet someone that showed promising characteristics.

We officially met in fourth grade, but our friendship reached its peak in fifth. She brought something to my life that I had only been able to feel briefly in the past. We shared many interests and found ourselves mirroring each other when it came to our behavior and mannerisms. She was my best friend. She stuck by me when no one else did and listened to my problems when I had them. As we got older, we grew even closer. She held my hand through many things, including the period I got bullied at school.

At the start of fifth grade, a new boy started attending my school. From the get-go I could tell he wasn't the friendliest of people, but I never suspected he would target me. I was still very quiet and kept to myself, and until then, I never had a problem with bullies. Regardless, he treated me like trash. He started off with little things like bumping into me, so I didn't realize it at first, but then he started calling me out by name. Even though I'm African American, due to my light skin, he'd often refer to me as a cracker, and other times just called me white. Despite the fact that I did nothing to him, day after day, every chance he got, he continued to persecute me. Throughout the year, he began accumulating followers in his hostile acts toward me, until, by the beginning of our second semester, he had an army of people willing to perform any task that involved humiliating me.

This army of his consisted of all the guys in my class. Most of which I considered my friends in the past. One of those guys just so happened to be my crush. Out of everyone in my bully's group of dimwits, seeing this come from my crush was the worst. Due to their vulgar comments and the treatment I got, compared to the treatment of fellow female classmates, I assumed they considered me to be unattractive and I started hating myself and school. At the time, I still didn't communicate with my family like I should've. I didn't tell any of my teachers, he was never punished and, therefore, never stopped. The only person I talked to about my situation was my best friend. She never told anyone either, but she did talk me through it. After talking to her, I'd feel better in the moment; in the long run, the effects of our conversations wore off and his attacks continued to rip through my confidence. I was left alone to take it on the chin. The only thing that kept me from falling apart was the bond between me and my best friend. But, as the year went on, she started evolving from the nice, relatable person I knew, into someone I could no longer enjoy.

Like most children, of course she was sucked into the universal black hole known as the internet. Not only were we not verbally communicating as often, she also started indulging in indecent content online. One night, while we were having a sleep over at my house, she decided to share her pleasurable online experience with me. And just like her, I was sucked into the black hole as well. Thankfully, after a few days, I realized that such inappropriate content was poisonous to a youthful mind, and I immediately found the exit to that black hole. Even though I still spoke to her from time to time, the bond we shared was left in the past. I was a little disappointed, but I moved on fairly quickly. The next year I found new, better friends. But of course, a new year meant new problems lurking around the corner.

Transitioning from elementary to middle school can be overwhelming and cause anxiety. Due to this fact, a lot of kids that are transitioning are insecure, and though the thought of finally attending middle school was exhilarating, on my first day, I was still accompanied by insecurities. In my case, I was more concerned with my physical appearance than anything else. As my hormones became more rambunctious, minor acne exploded into terrible breakouts and became much harder to keep under control. Going to school in my skin was hard, but regardless of my worries I beat the odds, and made it through my first day with my confidence unscathed. For a good while, my school days remained that way. As the year progressed, I developed more acne. It consumed my face and my confidence started to plummet. I started feeling ugly and worthless. I also had a strong, ongoing feeling that I was always being watched and judged, and all people could see were the things growing on my face. I quickly went from being obsessed with my looks to scowling at the site of my appearance. I felt like an ugly duckling and it seemed that no matter what I tried, whether it was changing my wardrobe or doing something different with my hair, nothing sufficed. After doing everything I could think to do at the time, I was convinced that I would continue to stay "ugly" for the rest of my life. My acne was always on my mind, but when I would look in a mirror I would be plagued with feelings of worthlessness. I would often find myself falling down an emotional rabbit hole, that in the moment, seemed unending. Though I continued to endure the wrath of my acne, I had an amazing outlet that I'd acquired the previous summer.

Fortunately for me, I had been introduced to the world of acting by a colleague of my dad's, who was kind enough to pay for me to attend acting classes. I came to find that not only was I a natural at transforming into completely different characters, but I also found that acting opened up a new side of me that I wasn't even aware existed. It made me forget about any and every toxic thought that inhabited my mind. While attending the classes, I joined a talent agency, which gave me the opportunity to do auditions. My very first audition was for an independent film titled "Ruth." My dad was good friends with the writer/director, who was also one of the lead actors of the film, and he gave me a shot at the starring role. Though the original feeling that acting had given me didn't follow me throughout my sixth grade year, it still served as a great outlet for all of my pent-up emotions. However, even with such an amazing outlet in my corner, I still continued to suffer.

As me and my peers aged, I noticed a change in myself and my female friends. Not only were styles changing, but so were our bodies. Though I expected to see changes in the physical appearance of my female counterparts, I was still caught off guard. Everyone seemed to have grown overnight. I was very educated on what was going on, but I was very ignorant when it came to the rate at which this stage of development would take place. As our bodies developed, the males indulged in rap music and other things that featured the modern-day standard of the perfect woman; with that, the more we developed, the higher the bar rose. The guys in my class no longer chased after the pretty, cool girls. They began exclusively chasing the more well endowed. Of course, setting such specific standards for a woman of any age is toxic, but it's even worse when such a standard is placed upon young girls who aren't even fully developed. Due to this sudden spark of interest in shapelier girls, of course, the majority of us females were taken aback when hit with criticism on our bodies by our male counterparts.

This not only confused me, it also added to the corrosion of my confidence. Already suffering immensely from the acne invading my once crystal-clear skin, this was definitely the icing on the cake. I fell into a period of self-pity. Instead of occasionally looking in the mirror to admire my beauty, I would use that time to wallow in a sea of notably unhealthy emotions. Never did I shy away from letting my friends in on how horribly I thought of myself. It was almost like my high. I fed off the pity from others like a parasite. Once I realized how I felt was wrong, I felt even worse. In my mind I didn't deserve to feel the way I did while simultaneously justifying it because of how unappreciative I was of my circumstances. I felt worthless, and once again, it seemed I was falling down yet another bottomless pit. I developed an unhealthy habit of degrading myself on a daily basis, crying for hours until I was knee deep in a pool filled with self-loathing and hatred.

During these emotional periods, thoughts of my mother would resurface. I'd often spend extended amounts of time contemplating every detail I could remember about her. "Why?" I'd ask aloud, while proceeding to assume an answer in my thoughts. I often found myself taking responsibility for her faults. As the year progressed, my self worth continued to wither. I didn't know who I was or who I wanted to be anymore. My dress code embodied how I felt, mismatched and out of place. Just before I felt I might've completely lost myself, I was granted a life changing blessing.

My dad often took the time to talk with me about my confidence issues. He'd explain how the claims I made of myself weren't true and gave reasonable proof to debunk my claims. Though his talks played a big role in the recovery of my confidence, my outlook on myself was far too skewed for the effect of our talks to last. I also craved validation from those whom I felt had no reason or responsibility to validate me. Eventually, my healthy validation came.

A week after I auditioned for the independent film "Ruth," my dad sat me down, and with sincerity in his voice, explained that if I didn't get a part it wouldn't mean I was untalented. I looked at him and nodded, fully aware of what he meant, and ready to accept the news I assumed I was about to hear next. To my surprise, his demeanor slowly shifted as he told me that I had gotten the part for the lead role of the film. The news filled me with glee. Immediately after I was given the news, I jumped up and let out screeches of joy and excitement. I was overcome with emotion. I nearly cried. I was so excited. I felt that I had found the path set for my life, that would guide me the right way. Instantly, my confidence became robust.

I held my head high walking through my school's hallways, thinking about how incredibly blessed I was to be granted such an extraordinary opportunity. Not too long after I'd gotten the part, it was time to start filming. I stayed and filmed for three days. While on set, I was able to meet some very amazing people, like the director who also played my father in the film, Hosea Chanchez, and the woman that played his fiancé, Naturi Naughton, I got the unique opportunity of seeing their phenomenal talent in person, and even getting the chance to act alongside them. The best part of my whole experience had to be being in front of the cameras. It was almost like being transported into a completely new world. As the camera man yelled, "ACTION!" the world fell silent. Everyone around me, excluding those who were part of the scene, vanished. Once the cameras stopped rolling, it felt as if I had just woken up from a euphoria inducing dream. It was amazing! After filming in Detroit, though I was excited about my career seemingly starting to take off, that wasn't enough to deter the negative thoughts I had about myself from taking over my happiness as I came back to school.

Just weeks after I got back, my experience on set faded into memory. I was back to being so blinded by my insecurities, that it was nearly impossible for me to recognize all the good that surrounded my life. I started to focus very heavily on what I disliked about myself. I tried numerous methods in an attempt to hide my flaws or get rid of them completely. After I began to recognize the success to failure ratio of the methods I was trying, I gave up and instead, shifted my focus to having pity for myself. I would go into emotional frenzies, racking my brain for any little issue I could magnify and blow completely out of proportion. I'd swim further and further out into a sea of misery, until I could no longer see the shore.

No matter where I was, my confidence lagged like a deflated balloon. I couldn't even find refuge in the comfort of my own home.

After my mother kicked my dad and I out, finances were scarce, and we had no choice but to move in with my grandparents. At five years of age, I was introduced to the beginning of a decade's worth of fond memories and moments I'd grown up to look back on warmly. Little did I know, I was also being introduced to the origins of loathing and hatred that would begin brewing later on down the line. My first couple of years with my grandparents were spent learning how to adjust and cope with new, better circumstances. In about fifth grade, though my past never drifted too far from primary thought and occasionally tugged at my emotions, I was definitely in a better position than I had been. Battered and bruised, I seemed to have finally been rising above my demons, triumphant in my efforts to find light in spite of the surrounding darkness. But instead of parading around a bright, hopeful smile, my head hung low, weighed down by exasperation and rage.

My grandmother has always been one of the most important women in my life. I've always looked up to her. Not only has she been the closest mother figure I've had consistently throughout my life, but she's also a beautiful, talented, hardworking mother of three that has witnessed life through a broken lens. She's probably one of the most resilient people I know. What I find most fascinating about her is how, despite all she's been through, her attitude toward life never falters. Instead of allowing her hardships to fuel her rage and misery, she uses the unsavory image of who she could become to encourage and continue her path of good nature and patience. Unfortunately, a sweet disposition is often taken for granted, and my grandmother's case was no different. Growing up with my grandparents, I saw plenty of foreshadowing for the periods to come. Like the times I'd wander into the wrong room at the wrong time to find my grandmother sulking in a pool of her own tears, or other times when my line of focus would suddenly be obstructed by a loud exchange of verbal attacks. As the years went by and my comprehension of the world around me grew, I was heartbroken to find the reason hidden behind the crying I witnessed over the years.

My grandfather, Leon, the boy who never grew up to be a real man because he's too busy looking over his shoulder, crying over his past; the "man" who disregards everyone else's pain and conducts himself as if he's the only one wrestling with issues; the person that takes all his frustrations out on everyone; the husband that years ago vowed to love and cherish my grandmother till death do they part, is the monster that subjected her to years of emotional turmoil and pain. He continued to further disrespect her by mistreating her children and grandchildren. Even going so far as to mistreat her mentally disabled younger sister. For these reasons among other things, at times I found it very difficult spending so much time at my grandmother's house. My grandfather infuriated me! The sight of him, smiling, laughing, struck a match that lit this fire, that would be further fueled as I witnessed him add nothing but unnecessary stress and drama to everyone's life. After years and years of allowing his behavior to have such a profound effect on me, I finally realized something that gave me the ability to ignore him. Though he caused everyone around him to suffer, at the end of the day it was because he was suffering himself and couldn't bear to watch everyone else flourish.

Throughout the day he'd wear a guise, masking the agony he faced every second of every waking hour, grooming everyone to believe he'd recovered from his troubled past. As an alternative, he used those he claimed to love as an outlet, getting his emotional fix through mental and verbal abuse. This reassured me that while we may have to endure him now, we'll all be victorious in the end, while he's left trapped alone in his own despondent reality. By adopting this mindset, I was, once again, able to find comfort in my first real home. Finally, I had been released by one of the anchors that hindered my growth. Yet, I still found myself trapped at the bottom. I felt gagged, unable to call for help, because help meant weakness, help was embarrassing. Unknowingly, I began to mimic whom I hated the most and dressed up my internal battles with smiles and laughter, attempting to hide it from those I held dear. Though I had regained a place of refuge, I still hadn't gained the confidence that I'd lacked since my tender years. I found that the biggest challenge holding me back was myself. Implementing small increments of self-deprecation into my everyday life, my humor, my wardrobe, everything revolved around my insecurities. Subconsciously consuming my surroundings, until over time, it collected into a toxic concoction that continuously wilted my confidence. Though I still continued to face many challenges, I had an army of support behind me. Throughout the years, after watching different people fade in and out of my life, I felt unwanted and unstable. It seemed as though every time I allowed my emotions to latch on to someone, my grip wasn't strong enough to keep them in my life. My failure to comprehend why people were always leaving, coupled with the damage I had previously sustained during the custody battle, caused my trust in people to be stifled. I became very skeptical of anyone I developed an emotional attachment to, wondering, "will I ever see them again after this?" I cried over those I cared for the most, praying to God not to take them away from me. That is, until I was introduced to the community of people that had been quietly supporting me throughout this journey, watching my character evolve before a screen.

Throughout the years, my dad has surrounded me with amazing people, ultimately cultivating a village of supporters. With kindness, compassion, and selflessness they helped carry me safely through my chaos. Inviting me into their lives and claiming me as their own, my family had grown exponentially, making up for those I've lost and the tough times I've had to endure. Without their involvement in my life, many of the problems I faced previously, though eventually resolved, likely would've lingered longer. The support deterred my thoughts from going down a wormhole of despair, putting me at ease. They helped prove to me that I was wanted, ridding me of my monophobia and allowing me to value myself more. So, I'd like to thank you all for what you've done for me. You've all left such indelible marks on my life that I can't even begin to fathom how it would be without your varying influences. All the support I've garnered has carried me a long way, building upon the strong foundation my dad created for me.

Since the custody battle, my dad has done everything in his power to give me the best life possible. Through him I've been given the opportunity to have some amazing experiences. More importantly, he provided me with the attention and care I craved and needed. It took a lot for my dad to cleanse me of the residue left behind by my mother. I still had many unanswered questions and many parts of me were still tethered to the life I left behind. My behavior was atrocious and unpredictable. I was also unapologetically bratty and I'd often throw tantrums when things didn't go as I wanted them to. Despite the difficulties he faced, my dad continued to work with me.

He handled me with what I I like to be describe as a delicate iron fist, always explaining things to me while still maintaining a serious demeanor and tone that demands compliance. While he disciplined me, he also showered me with love, guidance, and reassurance. My dad put a lot of time and patience into cultivating our relationship until it blossomed into a beautiful anomaly.

With every obstacle I faced, from difficulties at school to the transition from a little girl to a young lady, he was there. No matter the circumstance, if at any given time I needed him he would always find a way to overcome the distance between us. Over the years we've become inseparable. Now I don't look at my dad as just a father figure, I also consider him to be my best friend. My dad has built a barrier of trust around our relationship, making it easier for me to feel comfortable communicating with him. Every movement, every breath, every decision I make, I convey to my dad. Over the years, he's managed to make any topic of conversation I've come to him with comfortable, which, in turn, made me relaxed and trusting.

With our introduction to social media, our connection gradually began receiving praise and support. People marveled at our closeness, applauding my dad's parenting as they watched him sculpt me into a respectful young lady. I went to school proud, boastfully expressing the dynamics of our relationship to my friends. I was not only proud of what our relationship had become, but I was also proud of our ability to uphold the standard we'd set. Though from the outside looking in, our father-daughter relationship may seem to rely solely on my dad's efforts, it has taken a team effort to keep our relationship from crumbling under the pressure of societal norms. Throughout the years, my dad and I have grown closer in the pursuit of keeping our bond strong and healthy.

Where once I was ashamed to be alienated from my peers, I'm now proud to be uniquely separated into such a beautiful, highly sought-after corner accompanied by my dad. Our bond has gotten me through many emotional and psychological ordeals. Brave and relentless, I commend my dad for his heroic deeds, which saved me from the villainous clutches of my mother and more. Though I couldn't be more grateful for all my dad has done, I still revisit the thought of my mother from time to time.

After a little more than a decade, the thought of her still taunts me. Fabricated moments lure me into a sense of false hope. My mind wanders to "what ifs" as I fall down a rabbit hole of memories, tailor-made to satisfy my fantasy. Other times, when thinking about her, I'm met with disgust. More often than not, the thought of her is accompanied by many questions. I often find myself wondering why? When I'm alone, my questions fall on deaf ears, and when talking to family members my questions are often met with speculation. Fortunately, with age I've come to gradually accept that no one other than my mother can truly answer my questions.

As I've come to gain more insight on my mother's background, I've adopted a new perspective. Due to the contrast between the life I once lived while in my mother's care and the life my father has created for me, I look at her differently. I no longer see her as a villain with no motive. Would I call my mother a person of quality? No. I would prefer to think of her as a lost soul who sought refuge in the faux comfort of drugs and alcohol, but only found self-destruction. Fortunately, the pages of my story book encompassed a hero in the form of my dad, but not everyone's story has a hero. My life could have followed many different paths, some of which lacked a happy ending. If my dad had lost the custody battle and I were left with my mother, I'd be another horrid facet of her. Despite the haunting image my mother has left me with, I still desire to see her again. She holds the key to my clarity, and though I may not be able to reestablish communication with her until I'm eighteen, my desire keeps my patience anchored. I'm willing to wait. Though my primary reason for wanting to reconnect with my mother revolves around gaining understanding, there are more factors that contribute to that desire.

My mother has caused my dad and I monumental pain, even after she'd been expelled from our lives, and yet, sometimes I still miss the idea of her. Though there are women in my life that have stepped into a maternal role, sometimes I still can't help but envy those with their biological mothers. The bond between a mother and her child is set in stone from birth. For nine months their bodies are vessels for two, their eyes lighting up with incalculable joy as the obstetrician hands them their beautiful creations. Watching others lovingly interact with their mothers, I've always wanted to experience what that feels like. I have no recollection of any moment I've shared with my mother that resembles those I envy. When trying to recall such a time, I'm met with a woman with long dark hair and a blank face. While the thought of having my biological mother in my life still intrigues me, at times I find myself lingering on what could've been. Despite those fantasies, my reality would have been grim at best had she remained in the picture. So, when I look around and take stock of where I am now, I'm grateful that I was fortunate enough to avoid such a dark path.

I've painted a picture with strokes of dejection and woe, but there's more to my story. My past experiences have helped mold me into who I am today.

As my fingers perform a beautiful dance on the keys, they tell their audience a story of the hardships brought on by my mother's treatment.

But they also tell a tale of my triumphs and those I met along the way to get me where I am today.

They've taught me how to be strong when luck falls short and times get tough. Through the lessons fate has forced upon me, I've developed a new appreciation for life.

Over the years, as I've come to understand my circumstances more and more, my grievances have dwindled, allowing me to enjoy a more peaceful state of mind and a fruitful life. Looking in the mirror, where I once grimaced with disgust, I now find myself grinning with delight, proud of how far I've come. Once a mere soul groomed by unworthy hands, I'm now an actress, an artist, and an aspiring writer. I love who I am and who I'm becoming. Though I don't plan on abandoning my roots, I look forward to getting the clarity I need to move on from this stage of my life. Until that time comes, I'm grateful for my blessings, I have an amazing family, endless amounts of support, and an amazing life. Though I have many more chapters to add to my story, in light of what I've been through, what I've seen, and what I've heard, I'd say this is a happy ending.

# QUOTES

" The first step in becoming stronger is acting on weakness

" The situation itself does not devolve into a plight, one's optimism simply erodes over time

" An overwhelmed mind often distracts itself with courses, creating obstacles that aren't really there

Unhealthy people often
leach off the potential of their
healthier counterparts

The more fervor brewing within, the
hotter the brew gets, in turn you
must learn the art of patience to
allow the brew to cool and reap the
benefits of the brew in its entirety

Self-exploration can be the most
dangerous, but also the most
rewarding exploration of your life

Success comes easy to those who
strive for little

"Let the darkness of your past motivate you to build a light for your future

"Confidence fostered in a sedentary environment is often a mask

"Inner happiness is impossible to achieve when external influences are being entertained

Your past is only a crutch when you hold on to it, using it as fuel to reach your next destination is different

We are only as capable as we allow ourselves to be

Adopt the mentality of the person you strive to be

"Our minds hold us back more than any other influences, break the chains you've tethered yourself to

"Life may be fleeting, but there's hope as long as your heart is still beating

"Your future is much akin to a destination, as long as we follow the directions, we'll make it to our destination

The code to life is balance, without it
your world would tip

Love is found in quality never
in quantity

The greater your potential, the more
support you'll need

"One infectious weed can poison a whole field of healthy flowers

"A fire left to fester will gradually grow over time, there's no shame in seeking remedies to an internal flame

"Monsters have many faces, those who are the most dangerous tend to be multifaceted, don't be fooled by a masquerade

" The last holds no bearings over a
   powerful mind


" Your achievements are not leaden by
   where you came from


" We mold ourselves not
   our experiences

" If you spend your days looking back,
you'll miss the days to come

" Don't let the guise of family narrow
your view of who someone really is

" Don't succumb to inconvenience,
learn from it

"Trauma can be your greatest enemy or your greatest teacher

"Some of history's most beautiful artifacts were found in the most unsavory environments

# AFFIRMATIONS

I am strong

I will push through

My obstacles do not define me

My future is bright

I am talented

Others' actions do not
dictate my worth

I am good enough

I am more than capable
of pursuing my passions

I have the power to
change my path

I can overcome my
internal struggles

I am not at fault for
others' mistakes

I am proud of who I am

I love my appearance

I deserve to be happy

I do not deserve the
consequences from
others' actions

I am not my environment

I am more than where I came from

My past does not dictate
my current worth

My mistakes do not make me
any less worthy of happiness

I am capable of being healthy
despite what I've gone through

I appreciate my self-growth

I love the person I'm becoming

I understand that I am
becoming and that is ok

I look forward to my future

I am not ashamed of
where I come from

I am not ashamed of
who I used to be

I don't need to compare
myself to others

I appreciate my body

I appreciate my mind

I have the power to do
anything I put my mind to

# JOURNAL

Bottling up your emotions is dangerous. The longer they're caged within your introspection, the more toxic they become. They feed off neglect. Ignored or left in confinement for an extended period, they'll grow to a size that surpasses the protective lining on the walls of your mind. Once they're gone beyond that threshold they'll infect those around you, using your friends and family as their new hosts. To keep this out at bay, there are a number of different tactics you could employ. The one I use is writing down my thoughts. I pour all of my emotion into a sea of words. My thoughts may not be congruent or finely tuned to suit the gaze of an audience when I write in private, but it's still a great vehicle to use to release my frustration in a productive way. So, when you're frustrated or your head hangs low due to stress weighing it down, I challenge you to redirect your thoughts from your mind to the paper.

Use your "weaknesses" as the building blocks for a stronger foundation. Write about the things that you feel work against you in your life. Poison does less damage to the paper than your mind.

_____

_____

_____

_____

_____

_____

_____

_____

_____

_____

_____

_____

We are our greatest opponents. Many times, we work against ourselves and unconsciously stunt our own progression. Write about the things you feel you may do to work against yourself.

_____

_____

_____

_____

_____

_____

_____

_____

_____

_____

_____

_____

_____

Our minds are power houses of information, they can perform miraculous tasks and overcome the mightiest hurdles. This includes sustaining its composure in the face of a past that taunts and belittles. Write about a time you overcame an obstacle born from past experiences.

_____

_____

_____

_____

_____

_____

_____

_____

_____

_____

_____

_____

We sculpt ourselves into the sculpture we want to be. The things we've witnessed or been through does not define the final product that is who we are. If you desire to stray away from the expectations of the land you were derived from, then you're capable of implementing the necessary changes to do so. Write about a time you doubted the extent of your capabilities and how you overcame that doubt.

_____

_____

_____

_____

_____

_____

_____

_____

_____

_____

Toxicity spreads like a weed. It kills all those within the surrounding radius. Being around someone that harbors toxic energy is detrimental to your own well being. Write about a time you had to distance yourself from a toxic person.

_____

_____

_____

_____

_____

_____

_____

_____

_____

_____

_____

_____

Inconveniences are nothing more than teach-able checkpoints riddled throughout our lives. Write about a time you learned from an inconvenience.

_____

_____

_____

_____

_____

_____

_____

_____

_____

_____

_____

_____

You don't have to originate from ideal circumstances to do great things. Some of the most breathtakingly beguiling artifacts excavated throughout history have been hidden in the brush of the most unsavory of environments. Write about something you wish to do that intimidates you due to your current setting or where you came from.

_____

_____

_____

_____

_____

_____

_____

_____

_____

_____

Many don't know where to start when it comes to ensuring significant progression through their life and to where they ultimately want to be. A good place to start is by emulating those you hold in high regard and aspire to reflect. Write about someone you look up to and what you admire about them.

_____

_____

_____

_____

_____

_____

_____

_____

_____

_____

_____

Mentally plagued people will always seek sustenance from those they envy for their mental stability. Write about a time someone struggling with their mental health clung to you in an unhealthy way.

_____

_____

_____

_____

_____

_____

_____

_____

_____

_____

_____

_____

Venturing outside of family and friends and reaching for the hands of psychological professionals is no shameful act. Mental health is important, and getting help is the first step in the right direction. Write about the time you thought about seeking mental health care and hesitated or decided against it.

_____

_____

_____

_____

_____

_____

_____

_____

_____

_____

_____

_____

Monstrous people tend to build a white picket fence around their true nature so they may still benefit from the amenities of a person of higher caliber without putting in the work to be a person of higher caliber. Write about a time you realized someone had been deceiving you into believing they were admirable when they weren't.

_____

_____

_____

_____

_____

_____

_____

_____

_____

_____

To compensate for what they don't have, some may surround themselves with a great number of low quality people. They'll bask in their company while enduring deplorable treatment or neglect because they're convinced that more of anything is better than nothing. Write about a time in your life when you were operating in this head space or of someone you knew who lived by this philosophy and explain the consequences you or them went through as a result.

_____

_____

_____

_____

_____

_____

_____

_____

_____

Self exploration is imperative to becoming the best version of yourself by means of getting to know who you are. An introspective journey is scary, but very rewarding in the end. Write about a time you may have neglected your needs in favor of steering clear of progressing further into your own psyche.

_____

_____

_____

_____

_____

_____

_____

_____

_____

_____

_____

Moving on isn't easy, but investing so much time in your past that you miss out on your present or future isn't fair to yourself. Write about a time you found it hard to let go of something from your past.

_____

_____

_____

_____

_____

_____

_____

_____

_____

_____

_____

_____

Your trauma can either decimate your livelihood or give you your greatest and most valuable gems. Write about a time you learned from something traumatic that happened in your life.

_____

_____

_____

_____

_____

_____

_____

_____

_____

_____

_____

_____

_____

_____

When you neglect to tend to your mental health, the issues that exist will continue to persist. The fervor that brews from this boiling pot of issues will continue to grow hotter until you develop the patience to sort your emotional affairs. Write about a time you became discouraged to the point of neglecting your mental health.

_____

_____

_____

_____

_____

_____

_____

_____

_____

_____

_____

When an obstacle blocks your path, don't allow what lies on the other side of the obstacle to get away from you. Find another way. Write about a time you gave up on something in your life due to the difficulties surrounding it.

_____

_____

_____

_____

_____

_____

_____

_____

_____

_____

_____

_____

Everything in life is about balance, without it, things would tip into chaos. Write about daily behaviors you exercise to balance your life.

_____

_____

_____

_____

_____

_____

_____

_____

_____

_____

_____

_____

Build off the darkness of your past, use it to pro-
pel you forward. Write about a time you used a
bad experience to motivate you.

_____

_____

_____

_____

_____

_____

_____

_____

_____

_____

_____

_____

At times the sheer enormity of your potential may become overwhelming. You may need support from others to manage everything you have to offer. There's no shame in that. Write about a time you needed help managing your endeavors.

_____

_____

_____

_____

_____

_____

_____

_____

_____

_____

_____

Life isn't eternal, but no matter what happens, as long as you work towards your goal, all hope should never be lost. As long as you're alive, the possibilities are endless. Write about a time you felt hopeless and how you overcame that obstacle.

_____

_____

_____

_____

_____

_____

_____

_____

_____

_____

_____

In many instances, our minds are the difference between us and success in any area. If you overcome the obstacles of anxiety and doubt, you'll live a much more fulfilling life. Write about a time when doubt and anxiety inhibited you.

_____

_____

_____

_____

_____

_____

_____

_____

_____

_____

_____

_____

_____

# CONCLUSION

The feeling I got when writing the closing of this book was one of sublime release. A release from the shackles thrust upon me by my mother and a release from the fear embedded in the trenches of my psyche. I've told you my story, now it's your turn to choose what you do with your take-away from it. The only thing I want every reader to walk away with after reading this book is the inspiration to write their own conclusion to their story.

# ACKNOWLEDG-MENTS

Thank you so much to my editor and publisher Ardre Orie. And thank you to Kathryn Mattus for walking me through the process of writing out all the essentials of a book. Also, thank you again to Ardre Orie as the founder of the company that helped make my dream of becoming a published author a reality.

# QUOTE

“ The ruins of the past can be
repurposed for a greater future

— ZADA N. LUBY

# ABOUT ME

My name is Zada Nicole Luby. I'm a daughter, a writer, an actress, an artist, and a fitness enthusiast. I'm also very passionate about helping others, which is partly what inspired me to write this book. "My Perspective" actually started off as an essay for a school project, but after my father read it, he urged me to write a full book. I agreed, embarking on my first true literary journey, and after years of emotional outpouring, I managed to condense my story into the book you've just read. I logged the very first keystrokes to this story at the tender age of fifteen, so it's still amazing to me that this has finally become a reality!

# MY
# SOCIAL-MEDIA

If you'd like to keep up with me and what I'm doing, my Instagram and Facebook handle is @ZadaLuby.